SHAPING THE EARTH

Julie
Haydon

Contents

Rigby

Wearing Away the Land

The surface of Earth
is always changing.
The surface of Earth
is made of rock.
Wind, water, and ice
wear away the rock.
This is called **erosion**.

Over time, wind, water, and ice wear away the surface of Earth.

3

Erosion can happen in many ways.

Wind, water, and ice can cause erosion. People can cause erosion, too.

Wind can cause erosion.

Water can cause erosion.

5

Wind

Wind can cause erosion.

When the wind blows
in a desert, it moves sand.
The sand is blown
against rock.

Over time, the rock
wears away.

The wind blows sand against rock.

Water

Water can cause erosion.

When a river flows, it pushes against the riverbed and banks. They wear away.

Over time, the river changes its path.

Water pushes against the riverbed and banks.

When waves crash
against cliffs, the cliffs
wear away.

Over time, the cliffs
and land change shape.

Caves form in rock made of **limestone**.

When rain runs into cracks and holes in rock, the rock wears away. Over time, a cave is made.

Rain runs into rock.
The rock wears away.
A cave is made.

Ice

Ice can cause erosion.

Glaciers are rivers
of moving ice.

When a glacier moves
slowly down a mountain,
it carries rocks with it.

The ice and rocks
wear away the land
under the glacier.

Over time, a **valley** is made.

Rocks and ice wear away
the land. A valley is made.

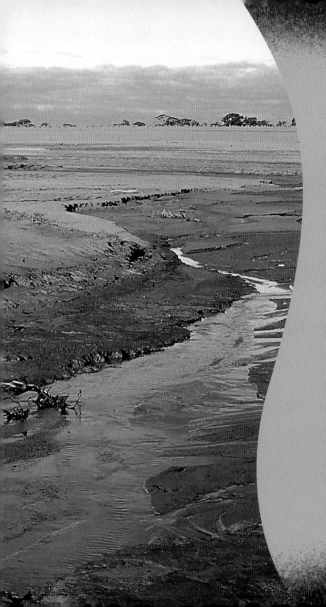

People

People can also
cause erosion.

People cause erosion
when they do not
take care of the land.

When people clear the land
of plants, the soil blows
or washes away.

This is called soil erosion.

Wind and rain wear the soil away.

When too much soil
wears away, plants
cannot grow.

We can help stop
soil erosion.

We can plant
more trees and
take care of the land.

Glossary

erosion the wearing away of the surface of Earth by sun, wind, water, and ice

limestone a type of rock that most caves are made in

valley a low area of land between mountains and hills

Index